COUNTRIES IN THIS SERIES

THE SIMPLE GUIDE TO

VIETNAM

CUSTOMS & ETIQUETTE

COVER ILLUSTRATION

Taking fruit to market on the Mekong Delta

ABOUT THE AUTHOR

GEOFFREY MURRAY has spent a quarter of a century in the Far East as a business journalist/analyst, including 16 years in Japan, five in Singapore and four in China. He has been decorated by the Australian Government for his work as a war correspondent in Vietnam, and has recently returned there to complete this book. His other publications include *Vietnam: Dawn of a New Market* (1997) and *Singapore: The Global City State* (1996).

Ancestral altar statuettes, Hanoi

ILLUSTRATED BY
IRENE SANDERSON

THE SIMPLE GUIDE TO

VIETNAM

CUSTOMS & ETIQUETTE

Geoffrey Murray

GLOBAL BOOKS LTD

Simple Guides • Series 1
CUSTOMS & ETIQUETTE

The Simple Guide to
VIETNAM
CUSTOMS & ETIQUETTE

First published 1997 by
Global Books Ltd
PO Box 219, Folkestone, Kent CT20 3LZ, England

Ⓒ Global Books Ltd 1997

ISBN 1–86034–090–3

British Library Cataloguing in Publication Data
A CIP catalogue entry for this book
is available from the British Library.

Distributed in the USA & Canada by:
The Talman Co., Inc., New York

Set in Futura 11 on 12 pt by Bookman, Slough
Printed in Great Britain by
The Cromwell Press, Broughton Gifford, Wiltshire

Contents

1

People & History

Halong Bay, northern Vietnam

What is Vietnam and who are the Vietnamese? The answers are complex. It is a country with an expanding but fragile economy, being developed by a battle-hardened people able to endure great hardships. It is a country whose government for years has epitomized to the West an ideological hardness, yet has also demonstrated the most remarkable pragmatism. It is a country built on fierce national pride, but at the same time is capable of demonstrating openness to new, foreign ideas, which it is doing to an increasing extent.

The Vietnamese have inherited many foreign influences over the centuries. In the north, a people forced to accept Chinese hegemony, either by paying tribute to the Emperor or having to accept periodic occupation, would then become strong enough to throw off the yoke of foreign oppression repeatedly only to have to face fresh foreign incursions once again.

A key exhibit in the Historical Museum in Hanoi is a record of these triumphs. Streets in the capital and Ho Chi Minh City (Saigon) are named after important historical figures who resisted the Chinese. Among these heroes are Hai Ba Trung (the Trung Sisters who led a three-year rebellion in AD40-43 before being killed) and Le Loi, who ended Vietnam's subjection as a vassal state of the Ming Dynasty and helped create the Later Le Dynasty (1427-1789) when traditional Vietnamese culture was able to flourish unfettered.

From China came the influences of Confucianism and Taoism and from India Hinduism. Buddhism, too, entered from both directions. Catholicism arrived in the early 1500s, in the shape of Jesuit priests from the Portuguese colony of Macao. Later, the French and Dutch caused the rulers of the Le Dynasty much concern, as they (rightly as it happened) saw Western missionaries as importers of subversive ideas.

Modern Vietnam began to emerge when land-hungry Viets spilled out of the crowded Red River valley around Hanoi before the fifteenth century, going on to defeat the Cham people on the central coast and colonizing the south in the seventeenth and eighteenth centuries. The Chams were a Hindu-worshipping people who had close links with Indian culture through trade and through the Khmer people of what is now Cambodia, and were virtually untouched by Chinese influences. With the advance of the Viets, however, Cham culture was quickly submerged.

A Vietnamese sense of identity was further honed by resistance to French rule from the late nineteenth century to 1954 – with a brief interlude of brutal Japanese occupation during the Second World War; finally, there was the struggle against the United States, which ended in the reunification of the country in 1975.

Family transport

Visiting Vietnam today, especially once the traveller has left the environs of the two major cities, where most of the economic development has been concentrated, it is easy to find evidence of backwardness and poverty. But it has to be remembered that the people of Vietnam have been at war, either overtly or covertly, more or less continuously from 1850 until 1979 (the invasion of Cambodia).

The French colonialists thoroughly exploited Vietnam's natural resources. Vast rubber, coffee and sugar plantations were established exclusively to serve export markets. Indigenous industries were supplanted in favour of imports from France. Crushing taxes and land requisition for the administration's favourites created a vast army of landless peasants for eventual conscription into French-run mines and factories both in Vietnam and in France itself. The exploitation continued during the Japanese occupation when Vietnam was forced to contribute food, cash and other resources to the Japanese war effort.

For a variety of geopolitical reasons, North Vietnam found its chief allies in the Communist world in its struggle to cling to independence after the Second World War. After final victory in 1975, a reuinified Vietnam followed the socialist model of the former Soviet Union, and this continues to exert a strong influence. Thus, Marx has been added to Confucius as a conditioning factor on national behaviour.

Given the historical background, visitors to Vietnam today will find a proud and independent people who do little to puncture the notion that they are special. They like to play up the 'David and Goliath' mystique to outsiders and perhaps half-believe it themselves. How else would they have dared to take on France, America and China?

Some writers have suggested that Vietnam illustrates the 'younger brother' syndrome. With a much bigger neighbour, China, it has been forced to display all the tenacity and seeking after attention, whether positive or negative, that typifies the behaviour of younger male siblings the world over. It may seem a bit fanciful but it is an idea that has some merit in explaining Vietnamese behaviour.

The bulk of the population occupy two bulges at each end of the country. In the south, communities developed along the maze of channels and canals that form the Mekong Delta, where the mighty Mekong River starting in China's Yunnan Province finally emerges from Cambodia and heads for the south. It brings down with it a great deal of rich alluvial soil that makes the growing of rice, and a vast array of fruits and vegetables, a relatively easy task. Thus, southerners have never had to strive hard to make a living, which has earned them a reputation for being lazy.

In the north, a similar pattern of colonization grew up around the delta of the Red River, which also starts in Yunnan Province and passes through Hanoi and reaches the sea at the present port of Haiphong, again depositing vast alluvial deposits in the final stages of its journey for agriculture to flourish.

But the north is also rich in anthracite coal and a vast treasure-house of minerals such as iron ore, copper, lead, bauxite, chromium, tin, tungsten and gold, along with fine clay for porcelain. Yet the people in the north have had to struggle much harder for their survival and have known periods of famine which the south has been spared. This has created a certain additional toughness in northerners, who tend to regard southerners as 'soft'.

On the whole, the people of Hanoi are thought to be more talkative and philosophical, but are also more elusive when answering questions. Northern Vietnamese are also somewhat more traditional and still hold the family and the longevity of old age in high esteem. Hanoians are also said to be a little more laid back and calmer than their somewhat frenetic southern counterparts for whom making money in any way possible seems to be a major preoccupation.

Temple courtyard, Ho Chi Minh City

It is said that if a Saigonese won a lottery jackpot of, say, $1000, he or she would most probably buy presents for their families, purchasing clothing, foodstuffs and other luxury items. Someone in Hanoi, however, would be more likely to feel that the money should be spent on necessities like 'fixing the roof' and 'buying new kitchen utensils'.

2

Legends & Beliefs

Young campaigner, Saigon

According to legend, Vietnam was founded as a result of a dragon's loneliness. It seems that the wandering dragon, an ancient symbol of good fortune, came upon a land of unsurpassed beauty. He then assumed human form, married the daughter of the local dragon lord and produced a son named Lac Long Quan. The latter, who is credited with creating an agriculturally-based, organized society, eventually married an immortal princess named Au Co and their union produced 100 sons born simultaneously from 100 eggs.

Because of the inevitable overcrowding, the family split up. Half the sons stayed with Au Co near present-day Hanoi, one of them founding the first Vietnamese dynasty, the Hung, some time in the first millennium BC. The remainder stayed with their father in the south, although eventually Lac and Au Co were to be reunited in the spirit world. Reflecting these romantic origins, the earliest name for Vietnam was Au Lac.

Whether or not a Chinese dragon did travel south, the fact is that real Chinese (from the start of the Han Dynasty in the second century BC) soon began to find their way through the protective mountain chain to begin a millennium of domination. Interbreeding followed which created the racial mix that became the dominant Viets. It is this cultural strain that survives, having almost totally submerged that of the Cham, whose Champa kingdom flourished in the south (centred on an area encompassed by the present-day cities of Hue and Da Nang) from the second century AD until the mid-seventeenth century. Apart from the Indian and Khmer influences, the Chams, until at least the tenth century, also had close contacts with Java, with whose people they shared important ethnic links.

The Hinduism of the Chams later became blended with Islamic beliefs, brought in by the Arab traders for whom Vietnam was a regular stop on their travels to China, along with some aspects of animism. Some of the remaining Chams and ethnic Khmers are Muslim today, although in a somewhat diluted form.

Catholic refugees fled south when the country was last partitioned, fearing oppression under the new Communist rulers because of Christianity's connections with Western powers. It was a fear actively encouraged by the US-supported South Vietnamese government seeking a staunch anti-Communist bloc. Catholics now constitute an estimated 10 per cent of the population, primarily located in and around Ho Chi Minh City (Saigon). Despite their fears, the Catholics have been able to continue to practise their faith, although there are some restrictions on the import of religious material and proselytizing is discouraged.

Buddhism is represented in two main forms reflecting the country's historic development. In the north, the predominant sect is Mahayana which developed in China and Japan before being brought south. The Khmers, many of whom settled in the Mekong Delta when the area was part of the dominant Khmer (Cambodian) kingdom, brought with them the Theravada form of Buddhism which represents the Indian influence. Also found in the south is a small mendicant form of the religion.

There are two unique native religions which are worth mentioning. Opinion is divided over whether the *Hoa Hao*, set up in 1939, is a form of Buddhism or not. Its founder, known as the 'mad monk' by the French, created a simple form of worship which dispensed with the need of an intermediary – i.e., the Abbot (*bonze*) or the monks that one normally sees officiating in pagodas around the country – and it quickly won adherents in the southern part of the country. Unfortunately, in the 1960s, due to having dabbled too much in South Vietnam's political and military affairs, the founder was executed and the sect banned for some years.

Slightly older, and even more peculiar, is *Cao Daism* (Holy See), created by a Vietnamese civil servant in the French bureaucracy to bring together a delightful pastiche of Buddhism, Confucianism, Taoism, Christianity, Islam and ancestor worship under one supreme being, the Cao Dai. The group's symbol is a single eye surrounded by the sun's rays. It has a pope supported by female cardinals. The faith also boasts a bewildering pantheon of saints including Jesus Christ, the French writer Victor Hugo, Joan of Arc and Napoleon Bonaparte.

The headquarters of Holy See is at Tay Ninh, an 80-kilometre drive Northwest of Ho Chi Minh towards the Cambodian border. The Cao Dai, with an estimated two million followers, had its own army of 25,000 men up to the mid-1960s, when it was suppressed by the generals who assumed power in a bewildering succession of coup d'etats in Saigon.

Readers of Graham Greene's *The Quiet American* may recall the Cao Dai playing an important side role in the story, the author describing the scene in Tay Ninh as 'Saint Victor Hugo, Christ and Buddha looking down from the roof of the Cathedral on a Walt Disney fantasia of the East, dragons and snakes in technicolour'.

Hue mausoleum dragon

Whatever their basic religious beliefs, a large proportion of the population continue to engage in ancestor worship, reflecting the great importance Vietnamese attach to strong family bonds and the existence of the extended family. As elsewhere in the region, Vietnamese believe that the soul lives on to maintain a protective watch over those who follow in the family line. To neglect due care and attention of the soul is to condemn it to an aimless wandering around the Kingdom of the Dead, while inviting disaster upon its descendants. Due to the disruptions of the prolonged Vietnam War, in which millions lost their lives, it is feared that there are a great many lonely souls wandering around unclaimed.

Mainly through the family altar in the home, the death anniversary is commemorated by special ceremonies, as well as during the various lunar calendar festivals referred to elsewhere. Traditionally, families have sought to have a piece of land which can become the ancestral burial ground, and the care of the graves is an important duty for the descendants.

As in China, the birth of a son is important because ancient custom has determined that only a male descendant can fulfil all the requirements of ancestor worship. The growth of urbanization and the mass movement of young people away from the countryside to the cities in search of work and a better life is placing some strain on these ancestral links, but they survive for now.

Top Tip: Taoist Belief System

Despite the seeming modernization of Vietnam, especially in the cities, the majority of people still believe to some extent in spirits who must be placated. Within these old animistic beliefs are blended some of the elements of Taoism (*Tao*: The Way), the religious system extolling virtue and humility founded by the great Chinese sage Lao Tze in the sixth century BC and brought in by the early Chinese invaders. Through study of the Tao, one is able to gain insight into the mysteries of heaven and their influence on earthly activities.

Many superstitions and ceremonies have sprung up, although these can vary from one region to another. Astrology, geomancy (divination from the shapes formed by a handful of earth thrown on the ground) and numerology (study of numbers to forecast the future) all continue to play a role in individual actions.

Top Tip: Lucky Numbers

A person's lucky numbers depend on the time, day and year when he or she was born and are determined by a numerologist. As in the West, 13 is generally considered an unlucky number, as is the number three – hence it might not be considered propitious to make important new commitments or undertake a major task on the 3rd, 13th or 23rd of the lunar month; and never try and take a photograph of three Vietnamese together!

Nine, however, is considered lucky. Fortunately, it is possible to consult a lunar calendar to check for the right moment to take key actions.

3

Anniversaries & Festivals

Altar inside Cao Dai Cathedral, Tay Ninh province

There are eight official national holidays in Vietnam, of which the most important is *Tet*, the lunar New Year festival which usually falls between late January and mid-February. This officially involves a three-day break, but the anticipation and preparations are likely to begin at least a month in advance and celebrations can drag on for a week in some form or another.

*T*et is a time for visiting, with a great deal of emphasis on the sort of 'first-footing' practised at New Year in places like Scotland. All the family, business and social acquaintances tend to visit each other at some stage during the holiday. Astrologers are often consulted because the first person to enter the house on the first day of Tet sets the conditions for the household for the coming year.

*T*here is no reason why a foreigner should not be invited to make this important first visit, but it is important that he or she is aware of the significance of the action. It may well be better to politely decline if there is any suspicion that the invitation has been extended purely out of courtesy, especially as one probably would not want to take the blame for any bad luck which the family might suffer in the coming year.

Top Tip: Avoid 'Bad Luck' Talk

One should be careful to avoid speaking ill of anyone on the first day of the New Year celebration as this will encourage a year of bad luck. In traditional belief, the first sound heard on this day can also set the tone, a dog barking, for example, portends while a rooster crowing does not, although it is no longer clear why this should be so.

*T*et is a time for gift-giving, the presentation of envelopes (usually pink) with new bank notes (known as *li xi* in the south and *mung tuoi* in the north); this practice is also found in China and other countries of the region with large Chinese communities such as Singapore. The envelopes are usually presented to all children, and can also be extended to cover domestic staff, subordinates and anyone younger than the giver as discretion dictates. They should never be given to anyone older! The amount of money in the envelope does not have to be large, it being more of symbolic value in wishing good fortune to the recipient.

Gifts other than money can also be given, especially to business contacts, staff and family friends. The choice would probably lie with something that the giver knew was in short supply in the country but readily available back home. Money and presents from *Viet Kieu* (overseas Vietnamese) will also be pouring in to relatives left behind by the former mass emigrations, so that this is a time of year when Vietnam looks at its most prosperous.

This, incidentally, is not a good time to do any shopping, as heavy demand tends to push up prices. And anyone visiting Vietnam on business should avoid doing so before or just after the festival as it is very unlikely that appointments can be made or honoured.

In the work environment, staff should be given a year-end bonus and also allowed time off not just for the official three days, but perhaps longer, given the fact that many may wish to visit families in other parts of the country which is likely to be a time-consuming process due to the poor state of public transportation.

For many, *Tet* is symbolized by peach and apricot trees that each household purchases for decoration and which are thought to help in warding off evil spirits. Northerners tend to attach most symbolism to the pink peach blossom, while the yellow apricot is considered more suitable for southerners. Thus, if one is going to give such a present to an acquaintance, it could be advisable to find out his or her geographical origins.

In preparation for the celebrations, houses, especially the kitchens, are rigorously cleaned and repaired, debts paid off, sins forgiven, enemies conciliated, and everything done to appease the spirits and start the new year off on a good footing.

Traditional foods are cooked in advance, as these foods take time to prepare and it is not considered proper to cook during the festival. The most popular item consumed in large quantities at this time is *banh trung*, a sticky rice cake wrapped in a banana leaf and steamed for 24 hours. *Tet*, in fact, is a time when food and drink seems to be consumed almost continually from morning until night, so that a little pre and post-festival fasting may not go amiss!

Although Christmas is not officially acknowledged in Vietnam, traditional celebrations do occur in the country. Catholic cathedrals in Hanoi and Ho Chi Minh City are filled to capacity and beyond for midnight mass on Christmas Eve. The international New Year is a public holiday in Vietnam, but there are no special celebrations.

On 30 April each year, the anniversary of the liberation of Saigon in 1975 is marked by a public holiday. Most celebrations surrounding this anniversary are limited to government activities, although the holiday is welcome in that it provides a neat break from work, being followed immediately by International Labour Day (1 May), which is also a public holiday. Vietnamese often cele-

Mid-autumn festival of Hoi An

brate by spending the day at parks with their children, on a picnic or just feasting at home. Most offices close for these holidays, although many shops, restaurants and bars remain open.

The birthday of Ho Chi Minh, founder and first president of North Vietnam, which falls on 19 May is marked by official celebrations, but it is not a public holiday.

Another double holiday occurs in September. First is National Day, on 2 September when Ho Chi Minh declared the creation of an independent state of Vietnam in Hanoi in 1945. This is a good time to send gifts to business acquaintances, joint venture partners, government offices and ministries. This is followed on 3 September by the anniversary of Ho's death in 1969. Actually, he died on the previous day, but the announcement was delayed so as not to mar the National Day festivities.

Of a more cultural/religious nature, Wandering Souls Day (*Trung Nguyen*) occurs in August and is regarded as the second most important festival after *Tet*. On this occasion, as in other Asian societies, families may visit temples or pagodas to pray for the souls of the departed, both one's own ancestors as well as the dead who may have no living descendants to perform the duty. As in China, joss papers are burnt and special foods are cooked and offered to the wandering souls.

The spring counterpart to this commemoration, incidentally, is *Thanh Minh*, on the fifth day of the third lunar month (calculated from the date on which the moveable feast of *Tet* occurs), which is marked by visits to tidy the graves of one's ancestors and pray to them.

The mid-autumn, or mini-Tet (*Trung Thu*), a month after Wandering Souls Day, is primarily for children. Mooncakes are eaten, and the occasion celebrated with noisy and colourful street processions.

On the 10th Day of the 10th lunar month, people in many areas celebrate the end of the harvest. Whereas on *Trung Thu* the presents are given to the children, this time the flow is reversed. Apart from children giving their parents gifts, it is also considered appropriate in many communities for patients to express their thanks to their doctors and pupils to their teachers in a similar way.

In addition, there are also special days and festivals peculiar to ethnic minorities and specific regions that are reminders of the country's rich and varied cultural origins.

4

Town & Country

Ho Chi Minh City

Anyone travelling around the teeming streets of Ho Chi Minh City will quickly appreciate its biggest problem: too many people! Natural growth is swelled by an influx of peasants lured away from back-breaking work in the rice paddies in the hope of richer pickings.

The city authorities are now intent on easing the strain by building six satellite new towns to the east and south, each with its own industrial estate to keep residents from flocking back to the main city in search of jobs. By 2010, when the towns are due to be completed, the population of the southern conurbation is forecast to be over seven million. But in the actual city area, the number will have been reduced from well over four million to three million or so, which the existing and planned basic infrastructure should be capable of handling.

District One, the inner city area on the northern bank of the Saigon River, retains some of its old charm with wide boulevards and a mixture of graceful colonial-style buildings from the French era now beginning to be overshadowed by a new generation of towering hotels and office blocks.

From there, tree-lined streets stretch out to the suburbs, where the charm soon disappears. Streets are choked with a mass of traffic assailing the ears with revving engines and tooting horns from early morning until the small hours of night. Housing development follows no pattern, with homes in pleasing architectural styles jammed up against grubby, ramshackle workshops in an endless low-rise strip development.

Hanoi is slightly less frenetic. Conservationists are trying to preserve the best of the ancient old quarter of the 1,000-year-old city and the gems of the French colonial period. The small opera house built by the French in 1911 and still equipped with the original mouldings and red-plush seats, is being restored. Old French villas on quiet, tree-shaded streets are coveted for renovation as up-market offices and residences.

Built around a series of picturesque lakes, Hanoi then sprawls out over the Red River, where a dike now protects the city from the former threat of devastating floods, into the surrounding rich, flat countryside. Once outside the old city, concrete tends to rule, for the market economy has completely changed the landscape and officials are having trouble regulating the growth.

Whole districts of old buildings with a distinctive Vietnamese architectural character are being swept away to make room for modern developments, especially in meeting the demand for office blocks and hotels of an ever-increasing foreign business community, and new housing for a growing population now over three million.

The scars of American bombing during the Vietnam war have all but disappeared from the capital. The most famous reminder of that era that remained for many years – the so-called 'Hanoi Hilton', the jail where American pilots were kept as prisoners-of-war – has gone, to be replaced by a new hotel.

Vietnam offers a contrast between a 3,260 km coastline with a succession of stunning, almost untouched beaches (although suffering from city detritus dumped in the waters and washed up along the coastline) and natural wonders such as Ha Long Bay, where some 3,000 limestone islands in a vast array of grotesque shapes climb vertically out of the sea, to wild mountains along the Laotian border where tigers once freely roamed.

In the south, the best known resort is Vung Tau, which in French times was known as Cap St Jacques and was a popular weekend retreat for foreign residents of Saigon wishing to escape the steamy heat of the capital for more balmy parts. It was a pleasant drive of no more than 100 kilometres to loll on the golden sands and contemplate a delightful dinner of freshly-caught lobster or other sea food to be found just off the coast.

Later, it was a popular in-country r & r (rest and recreation) centre for American and Australian troops during the war, and its port a key logistics channel for the vast amounts of equipment and food needed to keep the armies in the field. Today, those lolling under beach umbrellas tend to be local, while the city is the headquarters of a vast offshore oil-drilling programme.

Further north is Cam Ranh Bay, a giant US naval and air base during the war, subsequently used by the Russian navy, which boasts an outstanding beach, as does Nha Trang, whose numerous offshore islands offer good opportunities for fishermen and divers.

Da Nang also looms large in any history of the Vietnam War as a key military logistics site and the place (China Beach, several miles long) where American marines stormed ashore in 1965 to mark an escalating and ultimately disastrous US military involvement in the Vietnamese conflict. Just inland are the five stone hills and caves of Marble Mountain, sacred alike to the Chams, Buddhists and Viet Cong guerrillas.

Further north is Hue, the former imperial capital (1802-1945) on the banks of the Perfume River, and a noted cultural, religious and educational centre. Hue suffered grievously from French military depredations in 1885 and again during the Tet Offensive in 1968, when the Americans had a bitter struggle to retake the city from Communist occupation. Happily, the much-damaged old Imperial City is now being restored.

Hai Van Pass

It is only 80 kilometres by road between Da Nang and Hue, but the route is a difficult one, climbing as it does over the notorious Hai Van Pass (1,172 metres). For centuries it was this mountain barrier which kept the Viets and Chams apart. Appalling weather conditions, with snap flooding and landslides, add to the driving hazards of an extremely difficult road covering some 20 kilometres on each side of the 'Pass In The Clouds'. Many truck drivers find it obligatory to present flower and incense offerings on the altars at the top of the pass and pray to the mountain god for a safe passage. Soon, this will be a memory when a series of three road tunnels creates a straight route under the pass.

The central coastal region from the beautiful beaches of Phan Thiet up to the Ben Hai River, marking the dividing line between North and South Vietnam until 1975, also contains many relics of the Champa empire.

Top Tip: Tigers and Highlands

In sharp contrast to the hot and humid coast, are the cool, fresh mountains of the Central Highlands, where rich volcanic soil has nurtured some of the country's best coffee plantations. There are four principal towns worth visiting – Da Lat, adjacent to an imperial hunting reserve of thick pine forests full of tigers, elephants and deer and a summer retreat for French colonial officials from Saigon, Buon Me Thuot, Pleiku and Kontum. The area is still populated by various hill tribes who manage to maintain many aspects of their traditional way of life, colourful dress and unique customs.

Various ethnic groups also occupy the mountains separating Vietnam from China in the far north. The areas are among the poorest in the country, but boast magnificent scenery and are worth visiting if one is prepared to tolerate an extremely difficult journey over poor roads lasting many hours.

At the other end of the country, the Mekong Delta's rich vegetation and maze of river channels and canals offers a rich and fascinating history, being the hiding place for political exiles and religious apostates, pirates and smugglers, and, latterly, Viet Cong guerrillas. The main towns are Can Tho and My Tho, within relatively easy reach of Ho Chi Minh City.

Less accessible, but worth visiting if for no other reason than for the wide variety of shrimps it breeds, is Ca Mau on the southern tip of the country. It lies in a vast mangrove swamp known as the U-Minh Forest, although wartime defoliation has destroyed some of the beauty of this wilderness area. From here, those with time can also explore some of the unspoilt nearby islands including Phu Quoc, noted for its fine beaches and the quality of its *nuoc mam* fish sauce. More sinister is the former penal colony island of Con Son, where prisoners were kept in cages in appalling conditions.

5

Travel Tips

The bus into town

For the moment, most of the still limited number of foreign tourists arrive in Vietnam looking to revive or exorcise wartime memories, or searching for history, rather than seeking sun-kissed beaches or unspoilt and mysterious mist-enshrouded mountain peaks – although these certainly exist.

Whatever the motive of the would-be visitor, however, the first thing which must be stressed is that one should not go to Vietnam with extremely high expectations as regards comfort and convenience.

The tourism industry in Vietnam is still in the fledgling stage. As money becomes available, the country is trying to overhaul its badly neglected, and heavily war-damaged, road and rail network. There is also a need for more qualified and better trained service staff and management. But this is only to be expected in a country where there was no service industry to speak of for almost a generation. In addition, although economic development is accelerating fairly rapidly, Vietnam remains a relatively poor country by most people's standards.

This may be one reason why foreign visitors tend to face a dual pricing system, having to pay two, three or even many times more for virtually everything compared to the local population, even though the level of service offered may be no different. This includes hotel rooms, meals, domestic travel, especially by air, tours, and entrance tickets to places of interest like museums and temples. This practice is based on the assumption that the visitor is rich and can readily afford to pay the inflated price.

Top Tip: Patience etc is a Virtue

The most important attributes needed when visiting Vietnam are a strong sense of humour, patience and calm.

Top Tip: The Cost of Appearance

Visitors learn very quickly that it can pay to dress down in Vietnam. Despite officially-set rates and tariffs, the actual charge for some services can depend on one's appearance. If you look wealthy, or 'executive', or show that you are an inexperienced international traveller, then the price tends to be high. A tourist looking less prosperous, perhaps carrying a battered rucksack, and, even better, able to speak a few words of Vietnamese, can often end up paying less.

Vietnamese are a friendly people who don't appreciate foreigners who want to keep their distance. Actually, by mixing with the locals and behaving in a simple, straightforward manner, one can often see and understand more about the country than those on group or package tours, who may well enjoy a more relaxing time but eventually leave the country feeling slightly disappointed that they have missed out on something important.

Following a recent construction boom, newly-built international standard hotels in Hanoi, Ho Chi Minh City and some other major towns are now facing a glut of rooms and severe shortage of visitors, with occupancy rates as low as 30 per cent.

Vietnam's first post-war international standard project in the south was the Saigon Floating Hotel, towed in complete on a barge from Australia's Great Barrier Reef; the initial, very successful five-year lease was renewed at the end of 1994. Since then, major hotel chains from various countries have moved into the four and five-star end of the market around District 1, the city centre, remarkably unchanged from the height of the Vietnam War, creating a total capacity of around 5,500 rooms.

Hanoi has a lot of catching up to do, but plans are in place to build 33 'international standard' hotels of between three and five stars, mostly around the capital's various very attractive lakes, providing a total of about 5,000 rooms by 1998.

Mekong riverscape

Both cities want more. Ho Chi Minh thinks it will need 21,000 rooms by the turn of the century, while Hanoi more modestly aims for 10,000. But none of the rooms now on offer comes cheap, and many visitors on tight budgets find it better to go to the main streets in search of the rash of 'mini-hotels'. With land costs high, these hotels tend to be tall and thin, typically one room wide and two deep. But the limited number of rooms available still offer most of the basic comforts, such as en suite bathrooms, telephone and television, and even a refrigerator.

What may not be on offer is food cooked on the premises. But it is easy to find a decent restaurant down the street, and many of the hotels often have an arrangement with a nearby establishment to have meals brought in for the guest, especially breakfast. Below the mini-hotels are even cheaper guest houses and rooms for rent which enjoy good business.

In travelling around Vietnam it is worth remembering that this is a country which in 1995 had an installed electricity capacity of only 3,500 megawatts, no more than 500,000 telephone lines and a crumbling road network of which only 40 per cent is paved. Much of the basic infrastructure development has been in the two main cities.

The railways are in a sorry state. Most of the rolling stock is either steam-driven Chinese locomotives or Russian diesel-driven engines dating from the 1960s which were sold to Vietnam some years ago by the Belgians. The train system that links Hanoi to Ho Chi Minh City, and provides affordable transport to a large number of people, has slowly got better. What was a 72-hour journey in 1989 now *only* takes 36 hours!

The continued relative slowness is caused by the poor condition of the track, lack of modern signalling equipment and the delicate state of locomotives and carriages that would not be able to survive anything above pedestrian speed. The same applies to the lines beteen Hanoi and the major port of Haiphong, at the mouth of the Red River, and to Lao Cai, on the border with China. But rail travel is only an option for those with a great deal of time and a strong commitment to 'experiencing life in the raw'.

Vietnam has about 10,000 kilometres of roads, most of which suffered from war damage and neglect. Forty per cent of them are rated 'poor' or 'very poor'. There are 8,280 bridges half of which are dilapidated. Upgrading and repair has begun but it will be years before a decent road network is in place.

At some stage, usually every few yards, one is confronted by an onrushing truck or passenger bus, both invariably heavily overloaded and leaning over at an alarming angle, which requires fine judgement in giving way at the last possible second to avoid a collision by inches. The wrecks littering the roadside attest to the fact that good judgement is not always present.

Vietnamese residents of Ho Chi Minh City warn that there has been an increase in street crime. The streets of Dong Khoi, Nguyen Hue, Le Loi, as well as areas in front of major hotels including Saigon Floating and New World, where many foreigners circulate, are favourite spots for pickpockets, other thieves and muggers, usually operating from motorbikes.

In the latter category, a motorcycle swoops down on an unwary pedestrian at the roadside. The pillion passenger snatches a briefcase or handbag (some of the best can also strip a watch off a wrist in a twinkling) and the motorcycle disappears into the traffic at high speed.

Foreigners in particular are warned to be very careful about walking alone in the streets at night, even in well-lit city centres. Especially at night is it inadvisable to travel by cyclo. Some visitors have been harrassed, forced to pay two to three times the agreed fare on reaching their destination, and sometimes mugged, after taking what they thought would be a relaxed way of seeing the city.

Hanoi

Petty street crime such as bag or necklace-snatching are also on the rise in Hanoi, which was 'crime-free' until 1994. Pickpocketing on buses has become a major problem as more people commute to town. When it comes to witnessing thieves in action, Vietnamese in Hanoi and Ho Chi Minh City apparently turn a blind eye, as it is none of their business, regarding crime as a social problem that 'society' (i.e. the government) should solve.

B egging is common in the cities and countryside, and sometimes it can be very persistent. In the south, the beggars tend to be war invalids, some of them with hideous reminders of the conflict.

Top Tip: Beware of Beggars

Swarms of small children tend to surround foreigners whether walking on the streets or sitting at an open-air cafe or food-stall. They will look so forlorn that it is tempting to give them money. But it should be remembered that many of these children work for adult syndicates who will pocket most of the cash. Begging may be merely an excuse for a robbery attempt.

A nother juvenile pest is the shoeshine boy, who seems to be everywhere in the country eager to polish those dusty-looking shoes. They can be very persistent. Should you decide to succumb, payment should not exceed 4,000 dong, or say 20 pence or 30 US cents.

6

Food & Drink

Baguettes

Vietnamese cooking, while possessing a unique style all its own, has also been heavily influenced over the centuries mainly by China, Cambodia and other Southeast Asian nations. Stir-frying, deep frying and even chopsticks, for example, were introduced from China about a thousand years ago and became firmly embedded in northern culinary culture at least. The southern part of the country has been influenced more by Cambodia, Thailand and India. But although the ingredients may be appear to be the same, southern Vietnamese food is more subtle and less overwhelmingly spicy.

Items like bamboo shoots, bean-curd, lotus roots or nuts, bean sprouts, chives, Chinese cabbage, water spinach and kale will be familiar to anyone who has travelled in Asia before. Vietnamese cooking, however, depends heavily on a wide range of fresh herbs to provide distinctive flavours which locals insist mark the cuisine out as separate from any other.

Vietnamese restaurants around the country range from the tiny, street-side *pho* stalls, offering a noodle-based soup which is standard fare for many Vietnamese, especially in the north, to full-blown, opulent operations targeting foreign visitors and well-heeled Vietnamese.

The soup in *pho* is normally made from oxtail or beef stock, lavishly seasoned with a variety of spices and herbs, including crushed chillies, ginger, cinnamon and star of anise. In the north, thin strips of raw beef are likely to be added.

Many hotels and restaurants specialize in providing a comprehensive, banquet-style meal, specifically aimed at tourists wishing to sample different foods from around the country under what might be delicately called 'controlled conditions'. Other restaurants cater to a more select clientele offering perhaps one or two specialities, but at a price.

Top Tip: Bread & Coffee French-style

The French occupation provides a legacy of wonderful fresh-baked bread. An excellent cheap and satisfying meal, for example, is a fresh baguette filled with salad, local paté, cheese, or, especially at breakfast time, just butter and jam. Even in the smallest towns and villages one can find vendors selling crispy bread rolls filled with ground pork with herbal seasoning.

A fondness for coffee is also apparent throughout the country, small cups of *cafe filtre* being especially popular in the south.

The more adventurous visitor, however, can plunge into the back streets of Hanoi and Ho Chi Minh City to discover hole-in-the-wall establishments that offer authentic cuisine at low prices. Language may prove a problem in such places, but pointing at what one's fellow diners are having is a good substitute. However, as fresh, raw vegetables are very popular in many Vietnamese dishes, in some of the less well-appointed eating establishments it would be well to ensure that these ingredients have been thoroughly washed.

Anyone familiar with Chinese takeaways will relish the Vietnamese spring rolls (*nem* in the north and *cha gio* in the south) filled with shrimps, vermicelli, chopped onion and mushroom, which tend to be thinner and more delicate than their Chinese counterparts.

Many sauces are provided with most meals, including soy sauce and chilli sauce. There is also the ubiquitous *nuoc mam*, which can best be

Vietnamese dishes

described as 'rotten fish sauce' and a bit discouraging for the first-time visitor.

Nuoc mam is indeed a fish-based sauce, unique to Vietnam and considered as essential accompaniment to most meals. It is prepared from various species of fish that are mixed with salt and then left to liquefy in wooden barrels for several months – the longer the brewing period the finer the sauce and the higher its price. It can be used alone as a dip, or mixed with garlic, chilli, sugar, vinegar and fresh lime, when it is known as *nuoc cham*.

Among meats, pork and chicken dishes are the most plentiful because both animals are bred in large quantities (unlike beef, which tends to be expensive for this reason). The best way to eat these is to find a restaurant where one can barbecue the meat over a charcoal burner, adding to taste from a vast plateful of herbs and vegetables invariably provided – comprising items such as lettuce, onion, mint, basil, parsley, plus an assortment of fiery red and green peppers – and then dipped in *nuoc mam*.

Western visitors accustomed to eating only chicken breasts, however, should be warned that in Vietnam, like China, one tends to get everything – bone, gristle and various internal organs of a dubious nature. In fact, some of the bits Westerners might normally discard, such as the feet, are highly-prized delicacies and at a banquet are usually given to the guest of honour as a mark of respect.

Especially popular in the northern winter is what is known elsewhere in the region by such names as 'steamboat' and 'Mongolian hotpot' and here called *lan*. A large bowl, filled with seasoned broth, is placed on charcoal brazier with meat and vegetables added by the cook or by each individual diner. Apart from meat, fish is also used and one of the best dishes of the latter type is known as *cha ca*.

Given Vietnam's long coastline, of course, fresh fish is plentiful and cheap. The giant prawns, cuttlefish and crabs are delicious, even more so if they can be selected live from a tank within the restaurant. Eels are also popular.

There is plenty of choice over what to drink with the meal. Locally brewed beers, often major brands produced under licence in Vietnam, abound. There are also domestic brands, the best known in the south being 333, whose notoriously heavy use of formaldehyde can result in a pretty nasty hangover. In the north, Halida is the most frequently drunk brand. *Bia hoi* or fresh beer is worth sampling in major cities. Wine is available in major urban centres and tends to come from France or Australia.

There are also some potent local liquors, notably a rice wine called *ruou de*, which is similar to Japanese sake and has the same lethal effect on the legs unless approached with caution.

Top Tip: Water Watch

Although it's just about safe to brush your teeth in tap water, it is not wise to drink it. In a restaurant play safe and order bottled water. This can be especially important during the country's regular floods, when the water is most susceptible to contamination. Ice is normally produced from purified water, but it is always best to check in advance with the establishment serving it. If there is even the slightest doubt play safe and drink your whiskey and water warm.

Drinking water provided by hotels is boiled and should be safe, but, again, it may be wiser to buy bottled purified or mineral water. The most popular of the latter is *La Vie*, drawn from a natural spring some 60 kilometres from Ho Chi Minh City by a Franco-Vietnamese joint venture. However, be careful when buying as many local imitators have sprung up using almost identical bottle shapes and labels to try and confuse the consumer.

When dining out, it should be noted that some restaurants charge an extra five to 10 per cent for payment by credit card. Tipping, however, is not usually encouraged, although some hotel restaurants add a service charge. Restaurant bills are also subject to government tax.

Eating out is a way of life, although more so in the south than the north. With many wives working these days, and homes tending to be somewhat small for handling visitors, foreign visitors invited to dine by Vietnamese friends or business associates tend to find this means eating in a public place.

It makes sense to form a large party in order to enjoy a Vietnamese meal to the full. The idea is that a large number of varied dishes, reflecting a full range of tastes and textures and cooking techniques, should be ordered and placed in the middle of the table for communal dining. Westerners who would normally expect to eat their food along with a bowl of rice, as happens in Japan for instance, will find that Vietnam normally follows the Chinese custom of serving rice at the end of the meal. But it is possible to ask for it to be served earlier in the meal.

7

Shopping

Streetside eating

When Saigon, the former capital of US-backed South Vietnam, fell in 1975, the new rulers vowed to transform what they saw as a 'reactionary and rotten' city into a sober bastion of socialism. To underscore their intent, they renamed the city in memory of their deceased revolutionary leader Ho Chi Minh.

But any foreigner with personal experience of earlier times in Vietnam returning today to Ho Chi Minh City will have little trouble adapting.

Commerce still courses through the city's veins. Smuggled television sets from Japan, pirated compact discs from China, fake Levi jeans from Thailand – everything is on offer in a city parts of which look increasingly like Bangkok.

It is said America shipped an average 2,000 tonnes of equipment to Vietnam every day of the war. Much of it was left behind when the last helicopters fled on 30 April 1975, and can be found in backstreet shops and underground markets. Down by the Saigon River in a line of shacks known simply as American Market one could equip an army with dog-tags, night-scopes, boots, flak jackets and even parachutes. On Dong Khoi Street or in Dan Sinh Market in the tourist district, dozens of shops get by selling GI pens, cigarette lighters and dead men's sunglasses.

Mini-helicopters made out of Coca-Cola cans and 'Good Morning Vietnam' T-shirts are brisk sellers on market stalls alongside supposed GI dog-tags which baby-faced vendors insist date from two decades ago. Most will want payment in 'greenbacks' – the dollar being the currency of preference.

Out in the Chinese district of Cholon, the business ethic rules supreme as it has always done. Areas tend to have their own product specialities which can easily be assessed as they lie piled up on the pavement outside the narrow shophouses that always seem to be jostling for air.

After years of drab, Soviet-bloc-standard consumer durables, Vietnamese are looking for a change and keeping their eye open for quality. This tends to result in American products being number one, European number two and Asian countries, number three, except in automobiles/transportation where Japan is number one.

Denim jeans, perhaps the ultimate casual Western fashion statement of all, are now officially made in Vietnam. Though bogus versions of Levi's and Calvin Klein jeans have been sold here for years, a Singaporean joint venture is now manufacturing the goods locally. Since 1994, a number of Western clothes shops have opened in Ho Chi Minh City. Their products are not cheap.

Purchasing power is also boosted by the fact that most Vietnamese own their own houses, usually do not take holidays, do not pay for superannuation and have hardly any tax or insurance payments to fulfil. In addition, the majority live as extended families – average households contain six persons – where income is pooled for major purchases.

But companies hoping to make their mark have to keep in mind Vietnam's cultural, historical, geographical and religious differences which have different influences than those of modern Western markets. Since Hanoians have less money to spend, they still tend to purchase cheaper, but essential consumer goods, while Saigonese are already beginning to purchase 'big ticket' items such as motorcycles, cars and cellular phones.

One of the most noticeable differences between Hanoians and Saigonese consumers is their perception of advertisements. For example, if a television commercial is not directly product-related, the Saigonese tend to dismiss it, saying: 'What does this commercial have to do with the product?' Any unrealistic portrayal of a product will raise doubts as to the sincerity and quality of the market and thus jeopardize its marketability.

In contrast, Hanoians seem to enjoy television commercials for their sheer entertainment value. This could be due to the poor variety of entertainment available in the North. So long as a commercial does not attack their family values, the commercial will be seen on the whole as suitable.

Cham sculpture, Da Nang

The presence of the French and then the Americans played a significant role in altering

57

Southern Vietnamese desires, expectations and purchasing habits. Branding of product names into the consciousness of the Saigonese seems to have achieved much greater penetration than in Hanoi. Saigonese are aware of branding and have already made the association of brand name with high quality – such as having a Sony or Honda Dream II motorcycle. As a whole, Saigonese have more exposure to foreign products than the rest of the country.

The North has only just begun to understand branding. For example, they identify a Sony product with top quality but are still largely unaware of other brand names. Today, branding in Vietnam is not so much a question of purchasing a product because of its name or manufacturer but rather where the products come from, as already noted.

Hanoians still predominantly shop in markets, largely because those involved in agriculture continue to represent well over 40 per cent of Hanoi's work-force, whereas only about 14 per cent of Saigonese work on the land. With the influx of mini-marts and bigger state-run shopping centres, southerners are getting more and more exposure to new products and choices for the moment.

In the capital, a memorable shopping expedition involves wandering through a labyrinth of narrow streets in the old part of the city, unchanged for many decades, where traditional trades were carried out, each in a designated area still identified by the names of the thoroughfares – Silk Street, Gold Street etc. Now, the predominant image is of masses of small shop houses, bulging with goods spilling out onto the pavement, primarily clothing of every description, electrical products, medicines and traditional arts. The streets are thronged from morning to night with a vast press of pedestrians, making movement by any form of motor vehicle extremely difficult. In the maze of look-alike streets running off at all angles, it is easy to imagine getting lost.

Top Tip: Take Your 'Essentials' with You!

For the foreign visitor, the shopping experience can vary. Some of the items one is accustomed to finding in the corner-shop back home may not be available, or, if they are, prohibitively expensive. Short-term visitors should plan to be self-sufficient in the basic essentials, while those planning longer stays tend to stock up on items in short supply during visits to neighbouring shopping paradises like Singapore, Hong Kong and Bangkok.

The Vietnamese excel in various arts. Lacquer-ware, ceramics, fine embroidery, traditional silk painting and woodblock prints are all items worth taking back home. Rattan furniture is cheap, although it is more likely to be bought by long-term residents rather than tourists. For the latter, Vietnam has an abundance of precious stones which can be turned into jewellery quickly and relatively cheaply.

Antiques are everywhere, but the visitor buying such items can run into problems when trying to export them. The law says no antiques may be taken out of the country, but it is rather ambiguous on classification of what constitutes a protected item. Therefore, it is best to check before buying.

Top Tip: Bargaining Business

In general, whenever an exchange of money for a good or service takes place, bargaining is the essential means of settling the price – although a fixed price system is beginning to emerge in areas frequented by tourists.

The Vietnamese are extremely tough bargainers and, with a vast fund of patience, it is very difficult for a foreigner to come anywhere near winning the game. If time is not a problem, it pays to shop around, and always be prepared to walk away if the bargaining process is not getting anywhere.

8

Business Tips

Antiques shop, Xha San

There is a general consensus that in seeking to do business with and/or in Vietnam, much stress and frustration, as they say, come with the territory. Above all, everyone – and that includes the Vietnamese side – has to learn to wait, to be patient. As was demonstrated in the Vietnam War, the Vietnamese are a people who can wait and wait to get a deal that is most advantageous to them. Westerners tend to expect action 'now'. This can lead to business deals being scrapped because the foreign side has lost patience in the protracted nature of the negotiations.

Sometimes, it seems as if the Vietnamese feel they have to behave this way in order to show their toughness and business acumen, especially given their limited experience in the international business arena.

Top Tip: Understand Confucianism

To understand Vietnam's business culture, one must first consider the culture of the country. Confucianism still permeates much of Vietnamese life in some form or other, and in business that can often mean extremely bright, go-ahead young business executives forced to show deference to the boss, who may have reached his position by patiently waiting for the years to accumulate rather than through the demonstration of any special talent.

Vietnam for years followed a socialist model designed by the former Soviet Union, and this still tends to exert some influence. The result has been a business culture characterized by extreme caution with drawn-out decision-making process.

The demise of socialism in Eastern Europe as a commercial model and the switch to the market economy has resulted in a kind of split personality; some managers cling to socialist practices while others energetically forge ahead. Also, there is now emerging a young entrepreneurial class whose methods are firmly rooted in the capitalist system. This group is often self-assertive and aggressive, and is predominantly concerned with short-term goals rather than long-term growth.

Given the strong sense of national pride and independence, foreign business people sometimes complain that their Vietnamese counterparts are suspicious and tough to deal with. This is not simply a result of centuries of foreign involvement, but also of the influence of Asian business practices where relationships are important precursors to business negotiations.

Since Vietnam has only recently opened its doors to the outside world, it is too early to make concrete predictions about the direction its business culture will take. However, Vietnam's Latinized alphabet and fascination with the West sets the stage for a migration towards Western business practices. The country has a remarkable ability to absorb foreign influence while retaining its character and the people are pragmatic – using what works and discarding what doesn't.

Top Tip: Don't Worry About Gift-giving

Business rituals in Vietnam are much the same as anywhere else, so that a basic combination of politeness and common-sense should see the business executive through a negotiating process without serious etiquette difficulties. Vietnamese business meetings tend to be relaxed affairs with less of the formality that one encounters particularly in Japan and to a lesser extent in China. Exchanges of gifts common in China do not seem to be part of the Vietnamese culture.

Meetings are an integral part of doing business in Vietnam, face-to-face contact being considered vital; few, if any, negotiations are possible by phone, fax or letter. Businessmen with a lot of experience on the ground warn that meetings tend to take a lot longer than you might anticipate, so it is not considered wise to fill the day with too many tight appointments, some of which might eventually have to be cancelled amid much embarrassment.

Shoe stall, near Long Bien Bridge

Business cards should be exchanged with every-one in the room on the initial encounter before any discussions have taken place. But unlike Japan, it is not necessary to be terribly formal (i.e. handing over the card with two hands accompanied by a deep bow). But politeness suggests you pause briefly to examine the card and then wait for the opposite principal to sit down before doing so yourself.

Tea-drinking is an essential business ritual as in other parts of Asia. Again, it is usually considered polite to wait for the senior member on the other side to begin drinking before doing so oneself. A few sips will be quite sufficient for politeness' sake, especially if you don't find the tea to your liking. You may be offered a cigarette, and although smoking is prevalent in Vietnam it is not obligatory to light up and a polite refusal will not be taken amiss!

Good communication is obviously of paramount importance. For a long-term commitment, it would be advisable to learn the language. If, however, you are forced to use a translator, in conversation always face the person you are addressing and try not to talk to the interpreter all the time.

It is considered a good idea to let your Vietnamese counterpart speak uninterruptedly for a stretch. The advice is not to question him or her immediately on points you think ought to be dealt with there and then. It is far more polite, and effective, to make notes, bringing up queries when it is your turn to speak.

One can be direct, without being *too* firm, even though the other side may not be. There may be many reasons why your Vietnamese counterpart cannot give a straight answer – including the need to check with his or her political masters – other than sheer negotiating deviousness.

Top Tip: Be Prepared for Serious Drinking

Entertaining is, as elsewhere in Asia, an important part of the business ritual, although it may not necessarily occur at the first encounter. However, at some stage, an opportunity will arrive to unwind and get to know each other better. Vietnamese banquets can be fairly riotous affairs, with a great deal of drinking, so it helps to have a strong head and stomach. It starts to get serious when the words *tram phan tram* (100 per cent) are spoken, indicating that you are being urged to down the entire contents of the glass at one go. Anyone with experience of the Chinese *'gambei'* (bottoms up) will know what this entails!

9

Social Situations

Reunification Hall, Memorial to Ho Chi Minh

The Vietnamese are a proud, independent-minded people. It is therefore very important to avoid situations where one might be suspected of displaying an outdated 'colonial attitude'. This could involve saying something that sounds condescending. Likewise with one's actions.

Vietnamese place a great emphasis on creating and maintaining social harmony. Thus, they may avoid unpleasant topics or tell 'white lies' in order to defuse a potentially embarrassing situation. It is often very difficult to get a direct 'yes-no' answer out of them. For this reason, the foreign visitor may find it difficult to understand when he or she has done something that is considered in some way inappropriate or even unacceptable. Then one has to become something of an amateur psychologist to look for clues in uncomfortable silences or lack of eye contact.

Speaking of direct eye contact, this is usually avoided in many social situations until the two sides know each other well. A Western man who stared at a pretty young girl would find her bashfully looking away, or perhaps even feeling indignant at this violation of all known rules.

Modesty is considered a great social virtue. Hence, Vietnamese will invariably speak in the most modest, self-deprecatory terms about themselves.

Age is vitally important because increasing seniority in years brings with it honour and respect. Therefore, in meeting a group of Vietna-

---

Top Tip: Watch Your Voice Level!

Raising one's voice or becoming angry is considered a sign that one lacks self-discipline. It all creates a highly embarrassing situation for the person being shouted at and should be avoided.

Vietnamese, like other peoples in Asia, place great stress on saving 'face'. They are very skilled in detecting the real attitudes of others through tone of voice and body language and react accordingly.

mese for the first time, it is important to pay attention to the 'pecking order' and seek to greet people according to their rank within the group, whether it be a business enterprise or a family.

Many Westerners are tactile by nature, but this can get them into trouble in a conservative society like Vietnam. It is considered highly impolite to touch anyone of the opposite sex, no matter how innocent the motive – even a little pat of encouragement. It is rare, therefore, to see even a married couple holding hands in public (although the more 'Westernized' younger generation in the big cities sometimes flout this convention).

Temple of Literature, Hanoi

However, physical contact between the same sex is considered quite acceptable as a token of friendship. But as many people believe that a spirit lives in the head and shoulders, these are two areas of the body best avoided.

Although, as we have seen, the Vietnamese often avoid giving a straight answer, that does not stop them asking foreigners very direct questions about their age, marital status, family background, and even how much the clothes cost that they are wearing. This stems from a natural curiosity about life outside their country which few of them have had or will have a chance to see. One has a choice of answering frankly, or turning the questions aside in a gentle, joking manner that will not cause offence.

It may take a little time to cultivate the sort of friendships that bring about an invitation to visit a Vietnamese family home. Depending on political, economic and social status, that home may be rather simple and cramped, with very limited privacy, which is why many Vietnamese prefer to take their foreign friends to a restaurant for a meal instead.

If one is invited home, however, take a small present, but do not expect to see it opened while you are on the premises. Unless the friendship is very close, it would be unwise to drop in on a family uninvited, thus causing embarrassment that the house is not tidy enough to receive visitors. Normally, it is not wise to make casual calls around lunchtime, as it is traditional for everyone to enjoy a small siesta after the meal.

Immediately on entering the house, the guest automatically will be served a drink, usually tea or perhaps fruit juice. One is not obligated to drink it beyond a few sips – an empty cup or glass usually obliges the host to fill it up again!

Top Tip: Dangerous Liaisons!

Romantic partnerships between locals and foreigners are not actively encouraged, but they do occur. But a Westerner should be aware that casual liaisons are frowned upon, and that one should not start a romance without the most serious intentions. A chaperone may well be considered appropriate for the couple in the early days of their courting.

If a relationship is permitted to develop and then sours, face may be lost on the Vietnamese side which will create a difficult situation for the foreigner involved when an angry family comes a-calling.

10

Useful Words & Phrases

Tai Chi

Vietnamese began life as a mixture of Thai, Khmer and Muong languages, but was then heavily influenced by China which provided the bulk of the vocabulary. From the 9th to the 16th centuries, the Chinese script was used for writing. But then, with the influx of French Catholic missionaries, a romanized version emerged called Quoc Ngu which finally became official in 1920. Not surprisingly, pronunciation is based on the French alphabet.

Like Chinese, it is a heavily tonal language, creating all sorts of possibilities for the hapless foreigner to mispronounce a word and thus change its meaning, to the delight of the natives. There are six tones in the north and five in the south, and a simple word like *ma* can, for example mean horse, mother, ghost, rice seedling or tomb, depending on the way it is said. (Do try the words and expressions listed below. Your efforts will be much appreciated. However, because there is no easy guide to pronunciation, it is better to learn as you go, with help from your, no doubt, admiring hosts!)

To add to the potential confusion, social custom also dictates different words to be used when greeting someone, depending on their age, sex and status, although the stumbling foreigner will almost certainly be forgiven any linguistic indiscretion. The various greetings are:

chào ông	to an older or important man (grandfather).
chào anh	to a younger man (brother, husband).
chào chú	to a man younger than your father but older than you (uncle).
chào bà	to an old or important woman (grandmother).
chào chị	to an older woman (sister).
chào cô	to a younger woman (aunt)
chào em	to a child, male or female; someone subordinate to you; or someone close, such as a husband or very good friend.
chào bạn	to a friend of your age.

Useful words

Thank you	**Cám ởn.** The other person may reply **Không có chi** (You are welcome)
Hello	**Xin chào**
Goodbye	**Tạm biệt**
Excuse me	**Tôi xin lỗi**
I am very pleased to meet you	**Tôi rất hân hạnh dược gặp anh**
Yes	**Phải**
No	**Không**
What is this?	**Dây là cá gì** (for an object)
Who is this?	**Dây là ai?**
I don't know	**Tôi không biết**
I don't understand	**Tôi không hiểu**
Maybe	**Có thể**
That's okay/no problem	**Không sao**
Please	**Vui lòng**
Already	**Xong rồi**
Where is the bathroom?	**Cầu tiêu ổ dâu?**
Go	**Đi đi** (used to brush off beggars or people bothering you)
bus station	**bến xe**
taxi	**xe tắc xi**
cyclo	**xe xích lô**
train	**xe lửả**
where is . . .?	**ổ dâu . . .?**
motorbike taxi	**hon đa ôm**
turn right	**quẹo phải**
turn left	**quẹo trái**
stop	**dửng lại**

Numbers

zero	không
one	một
two	hai
three	ba
four	bốn
five	năm
six	saú
seven	bảy
eight	tám
nine	chiń
ten	mười
eleven	mười một
twenty	hai mười
twenty one	hai mười một

Facts About Vietnam

Vietnam is an elongated 'S'-shaped country, 1,650 kilometres long and only 50 kilometres wide at its narrowest point. Covering almost 15 degrees of latitude, it goes from a tropical climate of perpetual summer in the south to a far north where freezing winters are not unknown.

Vietnam has a current population of some 72 million, of whom about 10 per cent live in two main urban areas, Hanoi and Ho Chi Minh City.

In 1996, the Vietnamese unemployment rate in the big cities was around seven per cent – about 2.6 million people – rising to nearly 40 per cent, or some six million people, in the countryside. The workforce numbers 29.5 million in the countryside and 9.2 million in the cities.

The Vietnam War resulted in an estimated one million military and another 1.5 million civilian dead. Sixty per cent of southern villages were destroyed; in the north every major town and provincial capital, along with main roads, railway lines, bridges, ports and industrial facilities were repeatedly bombed. Fifteen million people were rendered homeless throughout the country.

The Vietnamese declaration of independence drawn up by President Ho Chi Minh in 1945 is modelled on, and its preamble matches the language of, the American version.

In his younger days, President Ho Chi Minh briefly worked as a hotel cook in England.

The ethnic breakdown is Vietnamese (86.8 per cent), minorities (10 per cent), Chinese (1.5 per cent), Khmer (1.4 per cent).

Taiwan is the largest industrial foreign investor, followed by Japan, although the United States is catching up fast after a late start due to diplomatic relations between the two countries only being established in 1995.

Vietnam's chief exports are crude oil, minerals and coal (30 per cent), rice, rubber, other agricultural products and marine products (50 per cent), manufactured goods, mainly textiles (20 per cent).

The most popular family name, occurring almost 50 per cent of the time, is Nguyen, the title of the final imperial dynasty. The family name is normally placed first, followed by the given names.

WAR MEMORIES

About 40 miles northwest of Ho Chi Minh City, the reconstructed Cu Chi tunnel complex offers tourists a chance to crawl through the labyrinthine, claustrophobic network to experience the life of the Viet Cong guerrillas who hid there from incessant B-52 bombing raids during the Vietnam War. Similar tunnels have been opened up to tourism in Vinh Moe, Quang Tri Province, near the former Demilitarized Zone between North and South. There is even a firing range, at $1 per live round.

Parts of the Ho Chi Minh Trail – the legendary wartime jungle logistics route along the Laos and Cambodian border by which the North fed its war machine in the South – may be turned into a tourist attraction.

When the film *Indochine* starring Catherine Deneuve was shown in cinemas in her native France, it is said that the number of French tourists to Vietnam doubled in three months. For a modest $100 a night one can even stay in the suite she used at the Ha Long Bay Hotel in northern Vietnam during several weeks of shooting in the area – although the waiting list is a long one.

Vietnamese women after marriage continue to use their own name, rather than adopting that of their husband. There is also no distinction in the language between Mrs and Miss. Children, however, take their father's family name.

Some superstitions in Vietnam are opposite to those in the West. Thus, a black cat straying across your path or into your house would be considered unlucky. However, a dog brings good luck. To dream of a dead person or a fire is also considered as a portent of good luck. White is prime mourning colour not black.

Dancing was banned after the Vietnam War until 1986, but both the ballroom and disco versions have become popular once again. Karaoke is very popular.

Climate

Vietnam is a tropical country, with a monsoon climate, and high humidity. However, the country can be divided into two climatic regions – the central and southern region has very warm, humid weather throughout the year, while the northern region has a distinct winter season (October to February) with temperatures around 5-10 degrees C and a very hot summer season (May to July) when temperatures average 28-37 degrees C. Rainfall varies between an annual average 150cm in the plains to 200-300cm in the mountains.

Vietnam uses the Metric system of weights and measures; electricity supply is 220V AC, and traffic drives on the right.

The Vietnamese currency is the Dong (VND). There are 100VND, 200VND, 500VND, 1000VND, 10000VND, 20000VND and 50000VND notes.

Officially, tipping is not permitted but in practice it is still widespread.

Banks are open from 8.00a.m.-4.30p.m. Monday-Friday and from 8.00a.m.-12.00 noon on Saturday. Office hours are 7.30a.m.-4.30p.m. Monday-Saturday, but they close 12.00 noon-1.00p.m. Shops are open 7.30a.m.-12.00 noon and 1.00p.m.-4.30p.m. every day including Sunday.

Emergency phone numbers: Fire 15, Medical Assistance 14.

Index